Morihiro Saito

Aikido

ts Heart and Appearance

AIKIDO: Its Heart and Appearance

©1975 Morihiro Saito

All rights reserved including the right to reproduce this book or parts thereof in any form without written permission of the publisher.

Published by MINATO RESEARCH AND PUBLISHING CO., LTD.

MINATO RESEARCH & PUBLISHING CO., LTD.

Tokyo, Japan

AIKIDO — Its Heart and Appearance

© 1975 Morihiro Saito

Published by MINATO RESEARCH AND PUBLISHING CO., LTD.
Edited by   Sugawara Martial Arts Institute
             20-13, Tadao 3 chome, Machida-shi, Tokyo, 194 Japan
             Phone & FAX: (0427) 94-0972

Distributors:
UNITED STATES & CANADA: JP Trading, Inc., 300 Industrial Way, P.O.Box 610, Brisbane, CA 94005. *BRITISH ISLES & EUROPEAN CONTINENT*: Premier Book Marketing Ltd., 1 Gower Street, London WC1E 6HA. *AUSTRALIA & NEW ZEALAND*: Bookwise International, 54 Crittenden Road, Findon, South Australia 5023. *THE FAR EAST & JAPAN*: Japan Publications Trading Co., Ltd., 1-2-1 Saruga-ku-cho, Chiyoda-ku, Tokyo 101.

Third printing: May 1991

ISBN: 0-87040-345-1

Printed in Japan

Foreword

The Aikido population keeps growing every year. Almost everybody knows Aikido at least by name these days. Newspapers, television and a number of publications are contributing to its growing popularity. This is a really gratifying phenomenon. However, when thinking about the future of Aikido 20 to 30 years hence, we—Aikido devotees—must constantly watch its growth with a noncomplacent attitude. Such attitude is necessary because we must choose the optimum form and process of Aikido development in treading the path to fulfilment of the art. The task of getting the true spirit and accurate techniques of Aikido across is becoming increasingly difficult as the Aikido population increases, particularly in remote areas.

This book has been published to convey to the beginner the "heart and form" of Aikido in a simple and precise manner. We would be most pleased if the book serves to accomplish two parallel objectives — 1) further popularization of Aikido and 2) correct initiation into the art. We hope the book will provide a fruitful reading.

March, 1975

Morihiro Saito

Aiki Shrine

Aikido Founder, Morihei Uyeshiba
(1883 — 1969)

Master of Aikido, Kisshomaru Uyeshiba (left) and the author.

Contents

Prelude

When asked what Aikido is, it is difficult to answer the question in a few words. But when asked for whom Aikido exists, the question is easy to answer. The answer simply is that Aikido exists for those who ask for it. In a limited sense, the art exists for those who actually practice it. Among the Aikido trainees, there are those who, endowed with glibness, claim to know everything about Aikido. Their actual training, however, belies their words and is not commendable. They lack enthusiasm about their training. I prefer the opposite type. If one examines Aikido patiently for a long period of time, something is bound to touch your heartstrings. That something is presumably the true answer

to the question "What is Aikido?" The answer, therefore, varies as you continue to refine yourself. In my opinion, the answer is sort of an unwritten law which allows all kinds of interpretations but is something which is not forced on you by others.

In guiding his followers, Morihei Uyeshiba, the Founder of Aikido, discouraged questions and implanted in the mind of every trainee the attitude of using his own imagination and ingenuity. For the imaginative trainee, the Founder provided the answers through his bodily demonstrations which were so convincing. The Founder certainly was not hesitant and sparingly in imparting the essence of the art but put the emphasis of his teaching method on

encouraging the trainees to cultivate their own eyes for a deeper meaning of Aikido. Such method, however, is no longer readily available even if some peoply may desire it. There also may be those who have no access to competent instructors.

Aikido officially acquired its name in 1941. By that time, the Founder had studied and practiced all sorts of Japanese martial arts. In inaugurating Aikido, the Founder did not identify it with a mere consolidation of these martial arts. He created Aikido by compounding the merits of ancient arts with the "Principle of Aiki" and incorporating into it all the elements common to every martial art.

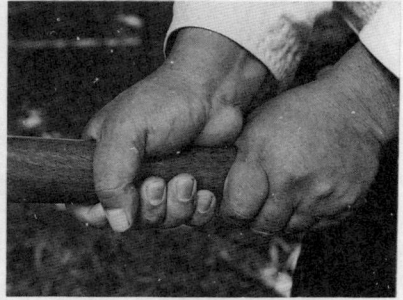

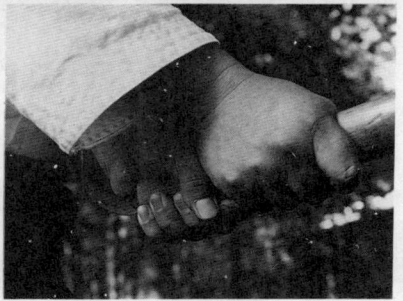

Consequently, it is possible to explain Taijutsu (Empty-handed exercise) in terms of Kenjutsu (Japanese fencing art) or vice versa. Both Taijutsu and Kenjutsu are integrated in Aikido. Aikido applications are so wide-ranging as to include the Jo (Stave) and Yari (Spear). Aikido may deservedly be called an ultimate martial art.

Aikido is unique in a number of ways, particularly in body movements and footwork. The forms of Aikido may be equated with △ (triangle), ○ (circle) and □ (square). △ means creativity, ○ means unlimited development and □ means a state of harmony. In other words, △ represents footwork and posture. ○ represents

harmonious circular movements without conflicting with your partner. It is a form of producing an infinite variety of techniques at Divine will. □ represents a form of integration with your partner and indicates a successful execution of a technique. Possible variations of □ are ⊿, ⊿, and ⊠.

A semantic analysis of the word "Aikido" dictates that in practicing the art, primary importance be attached to blending your "Ki" (Spirit) with your partner's. Intangible Ki manifests itself in the forms of △, ○ and □ which guide your partner's "Ki". If you realize this and train harder, chances are that your proficiency in Aikido will improve at a quicker pace.

For space reasons, Jo techniques have had to be omitted entirely in this book. Those who are interested in studying a whole spectrum of Aikido techniques are therefore advised to read a series of books (Vol. 1, 2, 3 and 4) entitled "Aikido — Coordinated Relationship Between Ken, Jo and Taijutsu", of which I am the author. These books, I am sure, will help you grasp the roots of Aikido which creates an unlimited number of techniques.

1 Training method

If the training method is wrong, even years of training will fail to produce desirable results in any respectable martial art. I therefore urge you to take due note of this point and adopt a correct training method.

A correct training method starts with learning basic movements, which are always practiced at each training session, and obtaining a prior knowledge of what these movements mean. Every time you practice, it is important for you to try out repeatedly what you have supposedly learned. Basic movements, which seem so simple and easy to everyone, are quite important in that they are usefully integrated into all Aikido techniques and serve to eliminate unnecessary movements and unnatural conflicts as a matter of course. Consequently, basic movements should be practiced at each training session and should under no circumstances be omitted. Such movements include "Body Turns" and "Training of Abdominal Breath Power".

In Aikido, "Ki" is considered critical because it is the origin of strength. Aikido training, therefore, is based on the concept of building up "Ki" power superior to muscular power. The meaning of "Ki" is extremely difficult to define. In terms of Oriental philosophy, "Ki" is inherent in every object in nature. No attempt has been made in this book, however, to explore the esoteric meaning of "Ki". I have only tried to explain Aikido movements according to the law of nature.

1. Basic information

• Manners

Bowing governs Aikido from beginning to end. Such courtesy is common to all martial arts but the one observed in Aikido is independent of others. A bow signifies a respect for your partner and yet must be made in a state of

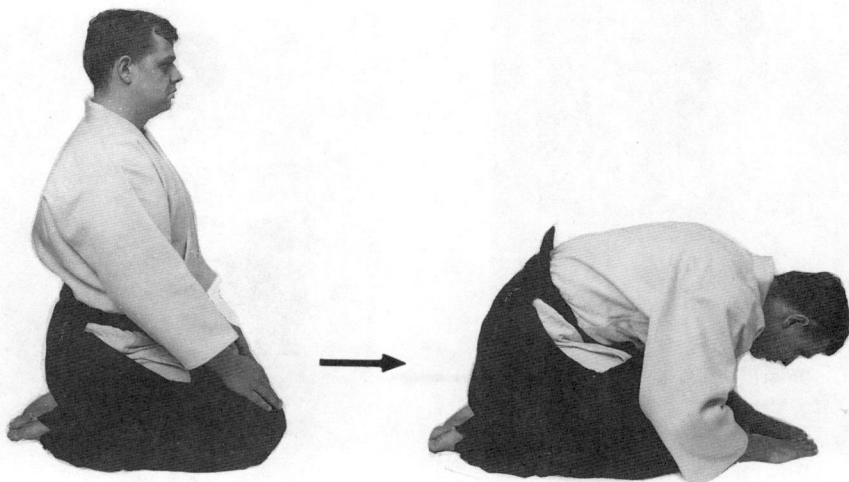

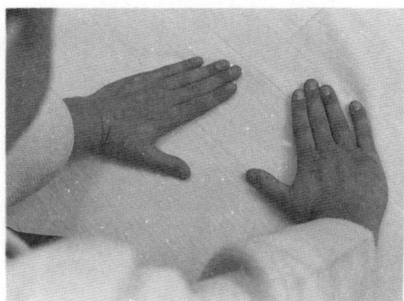

alertness. You are thus prepared to unleash any technique you want. You are supposed to be on guard every inch of yourself and ready to deal with your partner to your advantage.

In Aikido, in particular, bowing while standing has very much to do with standing techniques. Similarly, bowing while sitting has a good deal of bearing on moving on your knees and sitting techniques. In short, Aikido manners attach little importance to formalities but take up courtesy and behavior as a matter of spiritual exercise.

In making a sitting bow, form a triangle with your hands within shoulder-to-shoulder span. It is desired that you assume Hitoemi posture a moment prior to your partner's attack and be ready to counterattack like a cat. Your movement should be as natural as possible.

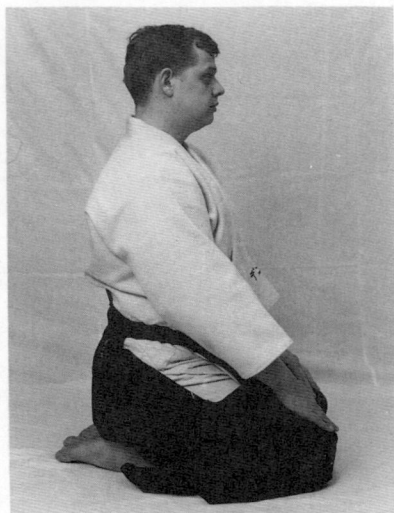

● Moving on Your Knees

This exercise is a walk on your knees without unbalancing the straight sitting posture. It is a repetition of right and left oblique movements. Turns are possible in any direction, with the posture remaining stabilized at all times. When you move your right foot forward, draw your left foot to its trailing edge. Your body is supported by your right foot, left knee and left foot. In this exercise, you

are required to relax your shoulders and lower your center of gravity. When you step your left foot forward, touch your right knee slightly on the mat, thereby maintaining a balance of the weight of your body. Please remember that this exercise calls for walking, not on knees but on foot. If you stand from this kneeling posture,

you will automatically be assuming an oblique stance.

Directional turns while moving on your knees are possible as in the case of standing exercises. There is a great need for making turns in Ura-waza (Turning techniques) and other techniques, as well as in dealing with a multiple-attack.

Top photo shows a turn rearward while moving on your knees. Note that only the knees are turned and that the position of the feet remains unchanged. Shown below is a turn of the feet, with the knees staying in contact with the mat.

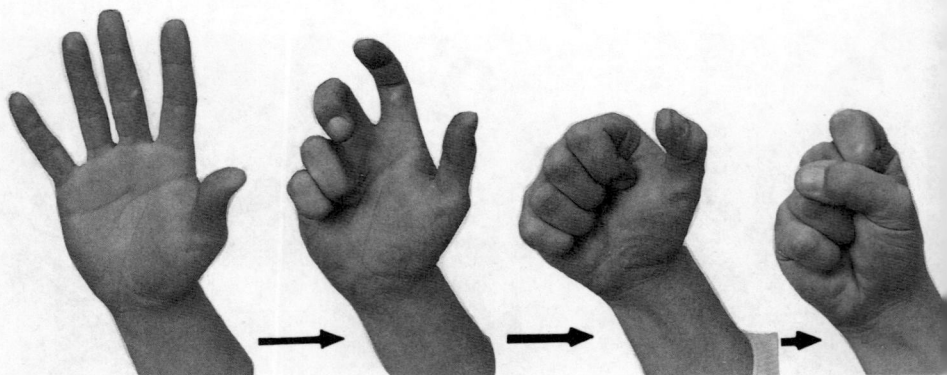

- **How to Hold Ken**

In holding a wooden sword, put your little finger on it first, followed by your fourth finger, middle finger, forefinger and thumb in a gripping pattern. Direct the tip of the sword thus held by your fingers at your partner and blend your "Ki" with his. Under such circumstances, your partner will find it hard to knock the sword down. This Ken posture is supple and yet hard in its inner core.

Katate-dori *(One hand held)*

Hold the hand of your partner in a Ken-gripping manner.

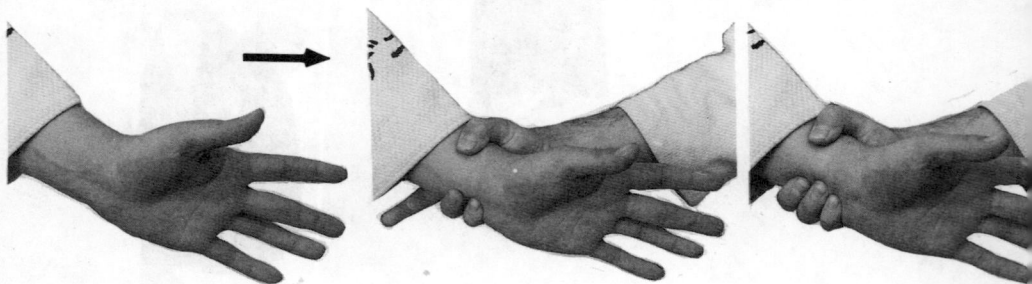

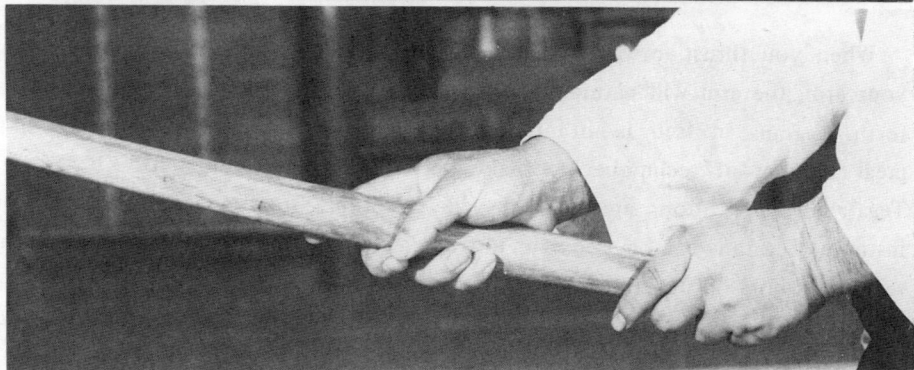

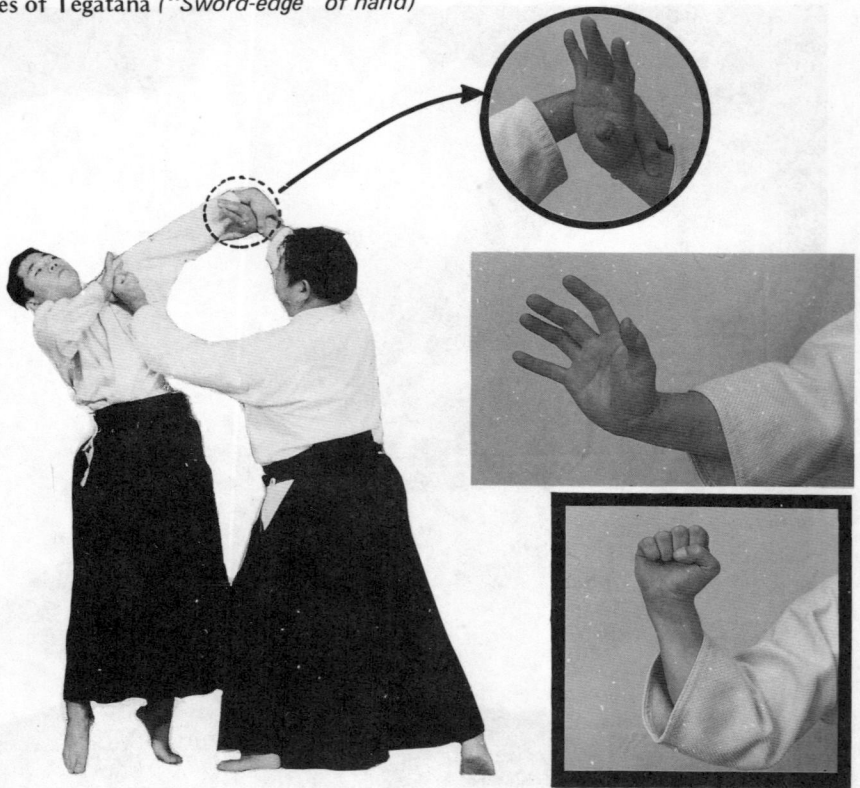

When you thrust forward the edge portion of your Tegatana without bending your arm, the arm will naturally form an arc permitting your "Ki" power to issue forth. Tegatana, in itself, is not intended for aggressive purposes. It rather is used in a great number of techniques to make better use of consolidated "Ki" power. Tegatana's applications are far and wide according to directional changes. For instance, Tegatana can be used as an instrument to hold down your partner's hand in securing a hold on it. Other uses include Atemi (A body blow prior to applying a technique), disengaging or unbalancing your partner's hold and gluing his hold to your wrist while swinging up your arm or sword.

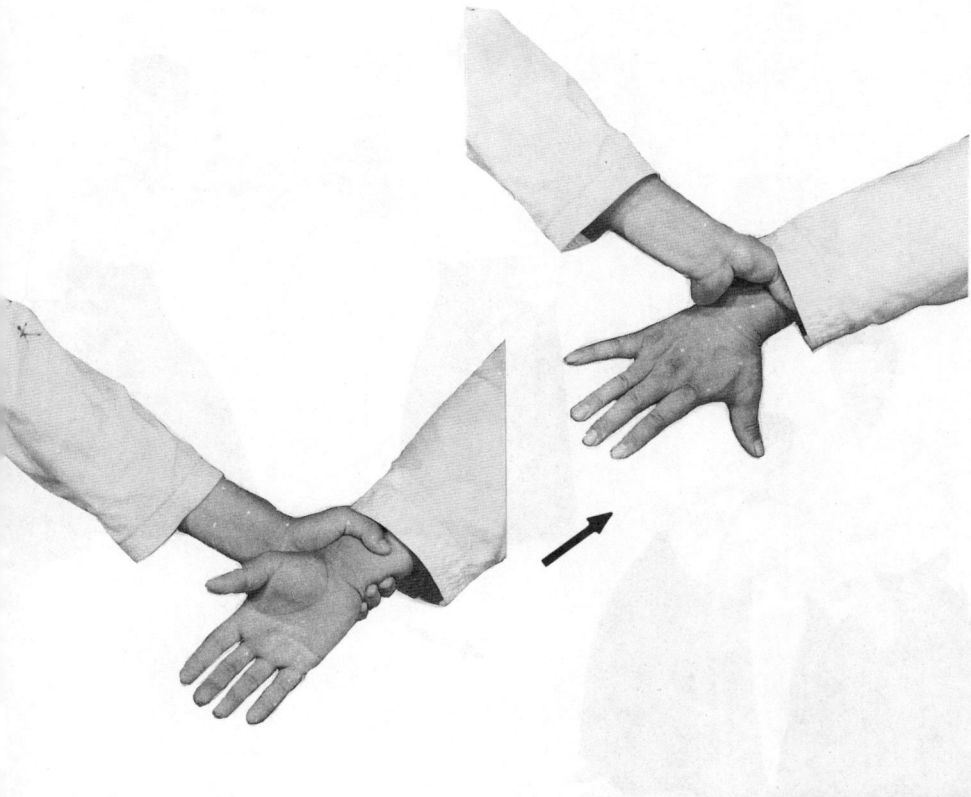

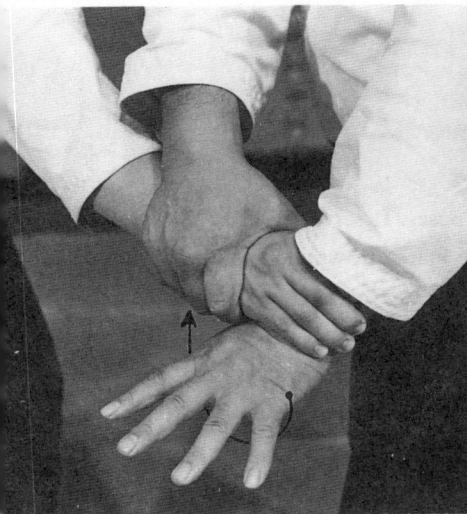

- Atemi

Atemi is not intended for destructive purposes. It serves to keep your partner's power in check and makes it easier for you to start throwing or holding techniques. There is a case, for instance, where you deliver Atemi to your partner's face and initiate a technique without giving him a chance to mount an attack with his hands. Photo shows how Atemi is delivered when your partner tries to hold your lower lapel. Note that Atemi synchronizes with the oblique turn of the body. Atemi should zero in on the most vulnerable spot of your partner.

When the distance between you and your partner is short, turn your Tegatana, jerk up his elbow from below and foil his thrusting attack while delivering Atemi at the same time.

Atemi must always be synchronous with your move to deflect your partner's attack. A moment of hiatus between parrying your partner's attack and delivering Atemi could result in his possible escape.

Atemi applied in Mune-dori (Lower lapel held) attack should be directed at your partner's face as in the Kata-dori (Shoulder held), Sode-dori (Sleeve held) and Katate-dori (One hand held) versions.

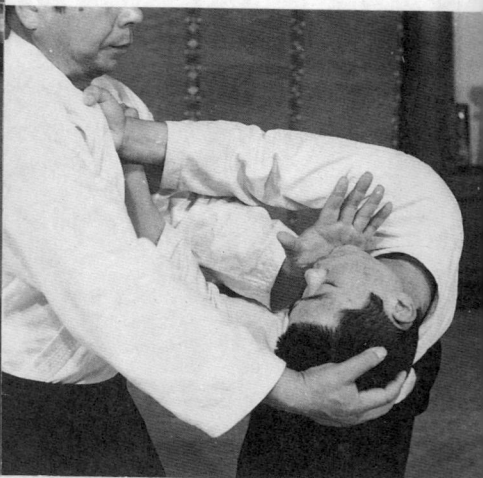

There are many cases in which Atemi, besides its usual function, is transformed into part of throwing and holding techniques. Atemi sometimes is deliberately omitted even when it is possible to deliver one. Those who have no knowledge of Atemi remain unaware of such omission. If you become overly Atemi conscious, however, you will lose smoothness in your performance. It is thus suggested that you learn Atemi as a matter of common knowledge in Aikido. But please remember that Atemi should never be omitted when it is essential. The photos should help you learn the extent to which Atemi should be exercised under varying circumstances.

There are two or three chances of delivering Atemi in one technique. Even when Atemi is omitted deliberately, you should know exactly when and where the preliminary blows are supposed to be delivered.

2. Basic movements

● Body turning

It is not difficult to turn your body when you are alone. The turn, however, is not easy when you have one of your hands held by your partner. Body turning is an exercise of keeping harmony with the strength of your partner and voluntarily stepping to his side in a circular pattern. In the exercise, you are required to let your held wrist stay where it is without pushing or pulling, charge your fingertips with "Ki" power and circularly slide to your partner's side with your toes aligned. Guiding your partner's "Ki" onward is an important process in quickening the whole movement. In this basic exercise, it is important not to let your held hand go astray outside your partner's line of attack.

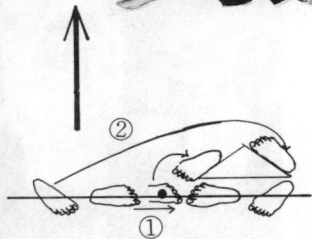

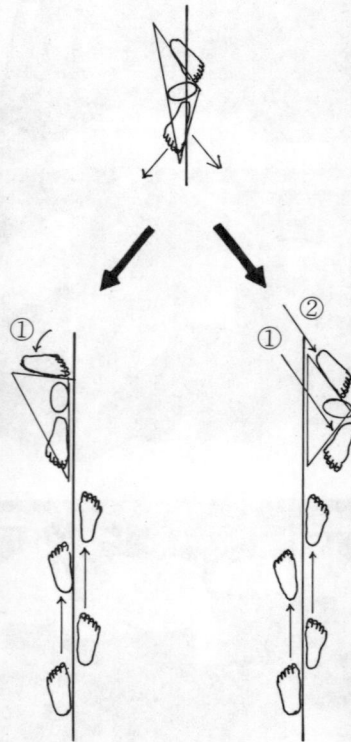

● Posture and Hitoemi *(Reverse tri-angular stance)*

The posture required in dealing with a sword-armed partner is a right oblique stance with slightly turned hips. In this posture, ignore the tip of his sword and his eyes. You must grasp him as a whole. Your posture must be flexible enough to allow movements in all directions — front, rear, left, and right. The diagrams on page 34 show movements to the left and to the right. The one at left shows the Hitoemi posture, with the left foot shifted in the desired position. The diagram on the right shows sliding to your partner's side on your right foot for a strike.

This is a body movement required to deal with Yokomen-uchi (Circular strike at the head). A continuous attack can be successfully brought under control by turning your body to let the thrust go astray, as illustrated here, following it up with an Irimi (Entering) technique.

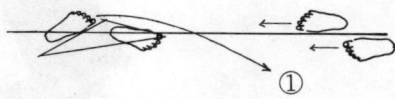

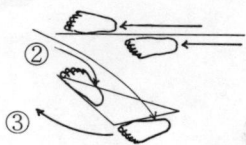

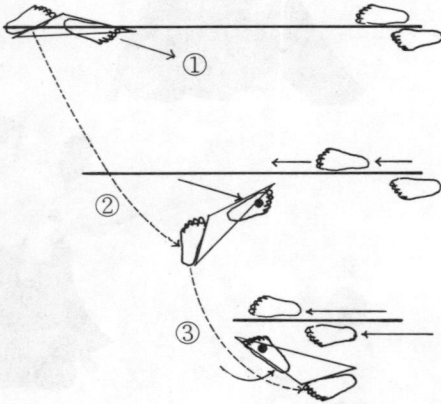

● Irimi

Irimi is an exercise of entering the rear of your attacking partner. This exercise bails you out of difficulties, not only in person-to-person combat but also when you are surrounded by many attackers. Irimi is more than entry in the rear. It transforms itself into Atemi, throwing techniques and Tachidori (Sword-taking), thereby providing an effective means of defeating your partner.

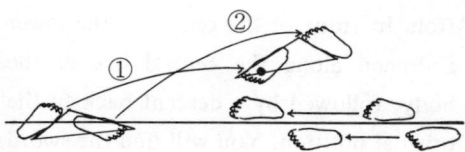

Suburi No. 1

This striking exercise calls for holding the pommel of the wooden sword with your left hand, swinging the sword up and above your head with your right hand on the forward part of the hilt and swinging it down in one breath. The swinging should describe an upward curb from in front of the center of the lower abdomen along the central line of the body, followed by a descent back to the original position. You will find the sword in place in front of your lower center of gravity if you start gripping it with your little finger, joined by other fingers at gradual intervals. In doing so, lower your hips fully in the prescribed position. Swinging the sword down straight is not as easy an exercise as you might think. You will discover this when you try the exercise in front of a mirror.

2 Aikido techniques

1. Aiki fencing art

Suburi No. 2

In this exercise, you are required to swing the sword fully upward and strike. Prior to the strike, draw your right foot back, turn your hips and swing the sword fully upward while staying clear of your partner's thrust or strike. Note that the upward swing is not a mere prelude to a strike but that it forms a posture of defense, covering your head against attack and diverting the opposition's move. The head is the easiest and most vital target.

Suburi No. 3

Point the sword vertically at the heaven above your head and breathe in deeply. Inhale the spirits of the Universe thoroughly into your body through the tip of the sword, integrate yourself with Nature and fill every part of your body with "Ki" power. Stop breathing after the inhalation for a while, lower the sword tip rearward and strike down in one breath. This is a really breath-taking Suburi.

Suburi No. 4

This Suburi features successive strikes at the left and right. In this exercise, your hips must stay in a lower, stabilized position regardless of whether your right foot or left foot is forward. The balanced use of the hips leftward and rightward in the sword exercise will have favorable impact on Taijutsu (Empty-handed exercise).

Suburi No. 5

This form of Suburi also highlights strikes in succession. What distinguishes this exercise from Suburi No. 4 is the fact that it covers your head against strikes by your partner and channels them off the target. It is desired that the movement of this Suburi be carried out smoothly and without interruption. This exercise is the so-called "deflective counteraction".

Suburi No. 6

Major functions of the Ken are not only cutting but also thrusting. Of particular importance is a series of cutting and thrusting actions. This particular Suburi exercise features diverting, in a flash, the power of your partner used in parrying your strike and thrusting straight against him under the path of his sword movement.

Suburi No. 7

Suburi No. 6 combines the striking and thrusting exercises in the same oblique stance. The No. 7 exercise differs in that the strike is launched from the right oblique stance while the thrust is unleashed from the left oblique stance. The thrust must extend forward from the center of the lower abdomen. In the thrusting approach, it is necessary for you to turn your hips, place yourself in Hitoemi posture and steer clear of your partner's line of attack.

- Matching of Ken

Matching Exercise No. 1

After sufficient training in Suburi, you will be taking the next step toward the so-called "matching exercises". These exercises will require one to two years to master. Matching exercises call for discerning the "Ki" of your partner from his overall entity and matching your "Ki" with his. In matching exercise No. 1, step to your partner's side on your right foot and cut him down in a most decisive manner. It is important, in this conjunction, for you to draw your left foot forward accordingly.

46

Matching Exercise No. 2

This exercise is based on Suburi No. 2.

Matching Exercise No. 3

This is an exercise designed to match your partner's continuous attack. Cut him down after the pattern of Matching Exercise No. 1 and thrust his throat in keeping with the up-swinging motion.

Matching Exercise No. 4

This is a provocative sword exercise, in which you take the lead in striking, diverting the parrying move and thrusting.

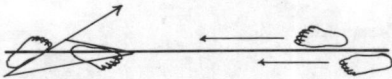

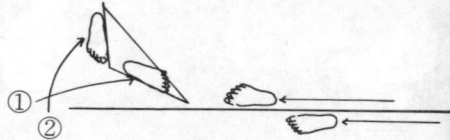

Matching Exercise No. 5

In keeping with your partner's striking momentum, control his right forearm (or head) with a "deflective counteraction" and bring the same part under control again as it tries to rise in a swinging motion.

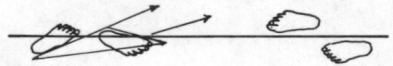

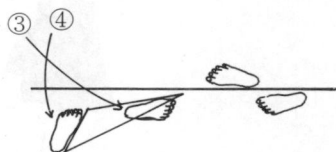

Matching Exercise No. 6

This exercise is an Irimi strike which is made possible by entering into the rear of the partner in a sweeping move. The deeper the entry, the better.

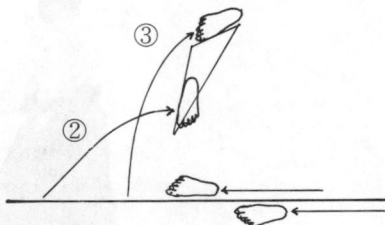

Matching Exercise No. 7

This exercise is a consecutive combination of similar exercises No. 1, 3 and 5. Because of its "Ki" linking series involved, it is called "Kimusubi-no-Tachi" or "Ki-Linking Swordsmanship" and is incorporated into Sword Partnership training.

What is important in training is to build you up by degrees. If you are at it diligently, you will acquire the desired strength naturally even when you are unaware of the proficiency you are gaining. On the other hand, if you are in too much of a hurry to master the art, you will definitely remain a faulty trainee and a slave to a bad habit incorrigible for a lifetime. This is worth remembering.

2. Kokyuho

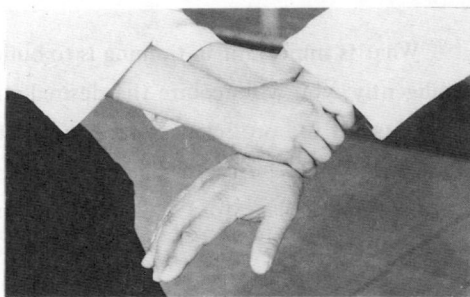

- **Standing Kokyuho**

Kokyuho is a method of building up your abdominal breath power, which varies according to the way your hand (or hands) is held and the directions of strength applied by your partner. This exercise therefore must be understood in relation to Taijutsu. Photo below shows the basic form of Kokyuho. Experiment with various "held" patterns and see how you could reduce them to this basic form. The basic form allows your partner to get hold of your wrist with both his hands from sideways. You respond to this by lowering your elbow and hips and circularly swinging to his side for a throw. In this case, do not bend your arm but make full use of your Tegatana. This Kokyuho serves to strengthen your hip turns which are most important in Taijutsu.

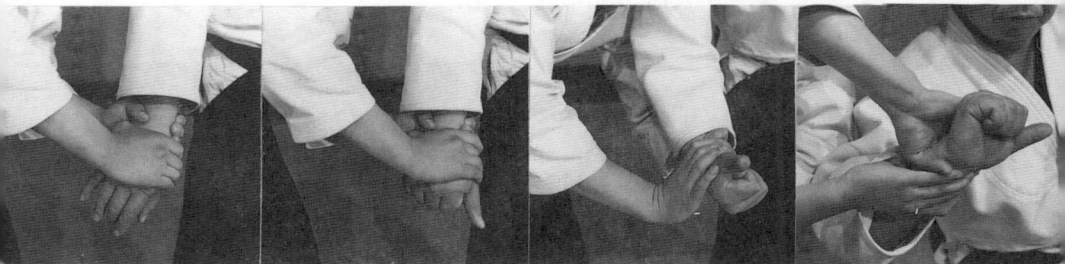

55

● Kokyuho against Two-Man Attack

The more the opposition, the more acutely you become conscious of your held wrists. To cope with such a situation successfully, you are required to swing up your arms and step forward while unbalancing the two attackers according to the basic form, turn your right Tegatana and draw them to you for multiple throws.

- **Sitting Kokyuho**

This exercise calls for your lowering your elbow, swinging up your Tegatana and bringing your partner down by forming a link between the center of your lower abdomen and your Tegatana. As he falls down, advance your knees to his side and control his "Ki" to sit up with your Tegatana. Even in the midst of this exercise, you must stay attentive and alert to your surroundings for possible attack from other sources.

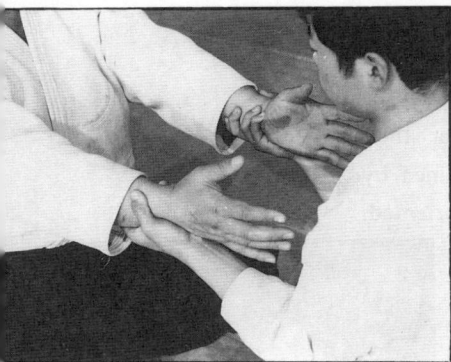

Sitting exercises vary according to [vari]ed circumstances. When held from [bel]ow, unbalance your partner by splay[ing] out your hands. When held from [abo]ve, buoy him up with your hips for a [thr]ow.

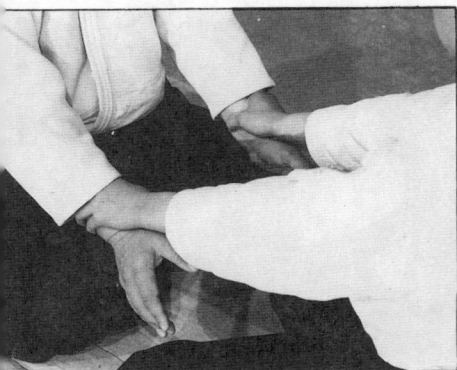

3. Holding techniques

In many cases, holding exercises are a logical gateway to pinning your partner down. Throwing techniques are sometimes concluded without any follow-up but at other times are followed by pinning. The techniques, which are going to be introduced here, transcend the categories of holding and pinning. Note that their emphasis is on what parts of the body are trained by these techniques. In other words, a training-oriented, noncombative approach has been given priority.

- **Dai-Ikkyo (Arm pin)**

Suwari-waza *(Sitting exercise)* : Shomen-uchi *(Straight strike at the head)* Dai-Ikkyo Omote-waza *(Front technique)*

Initiate a strike with Tegatana calling out your partner's "Ki", firmly get hold of his parrying hand on the pulse side and pin it toward his head. Bring his whole body under control by pinning his wrist and elbow.

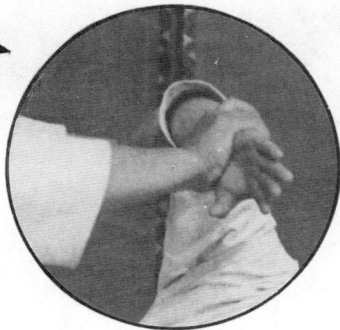

Tachi-waza *(Standing exercise)* :
Shomen-uchi Dai-Ikkyo Omote-waza

In the standing exercise, keep the right distance between you and your partner with your right foot, put him off balance by jerking your hips and thrust forward with your left foot to pin him down. Your posture must remain well-balanced during the whole exercise. It is wrong for you try, as is often the case, to pin your partner while letting your momentum circle his center. Always remember that it is your own center that should dictate the movements.

Suwari-waza : Shomen-uchi Dai Ikkyo
(Turning technique) Ura-waza

This technique requires you to align your knees, in the case of sitting, or your toes in the standing pattern, and circularly pin your partner down while obliquely turning your body. The holding method is the same as one employed in Omote-waza. In circularly pinning your partner down, the right thing to do is to stretch your hands and add to the pinning momentum an ounce of push and twist.

See to it that your right hand holds your partner's wrist on the pulse side and your left hand just above the joint of his elbow. What makes Dai-Ikkyo perfect is a correct hold on the prescribed areas.

Ushiro Ryote-dori *(Both hands held from behind)* Dai-Ikkyo

Particularly important in this exercise is the turning of your hips. You are required to unbalance your partner by turning your hips and pin him down while staying close to him.

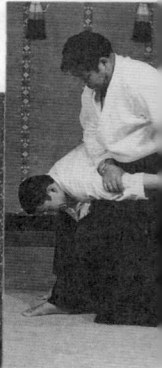

Starting with Shomen-uchi, Dai-Ikkyo evolves into a wide variety of exercises, including Katate-dori (One hand held), Sode-dori (Sleeve held), Kata-dori (Shoulder held), Mune-dori (Lower lapel held), Tsuki (Thrust) and Ushiro Ryokata-dori (Both shoulders held from behind). Such evolution makes Taijutsu singularly interesting.

Dai-Ikkyo Henka-waza *(Varied exercise)*

This varied exercise enables you to "glue" your partner to the mat in a flash. You are required to lead his "Ki", stay clear of his line of attack by obliquely turning your body and diagonally pin him to the mat. In this exercise, front and turning techniques are indistinguishable.

● **Dai-Nikyo** *(Wrist turn)*   ⇨

Shomen-uchi Dai-Nikyo Omote-waza

The pinning technique of Dai-Ikkyo has a common application in Dai-Nikyo, Dai-Sankyo (Arm twist), Dai Yonkyo (Forearm pin) and Dai-Gokyo (Defense against armed attacks). In Dai-Nikyo Omote-waza, cut downward your partner's wrist with Tegatana, hold the back of his hand and pin him down. Once he is pinned on the mat, advance your knee to his neck and conclude the exercise in the manner shown in the photo.

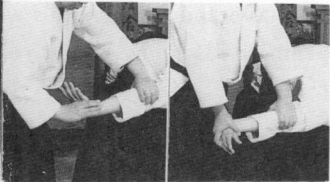

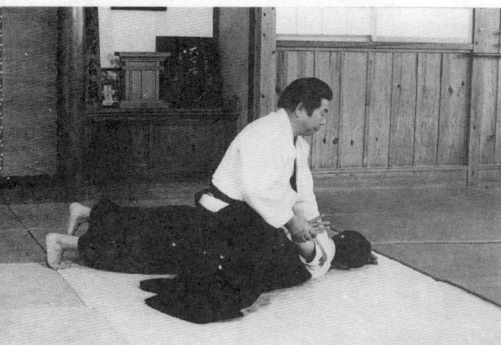

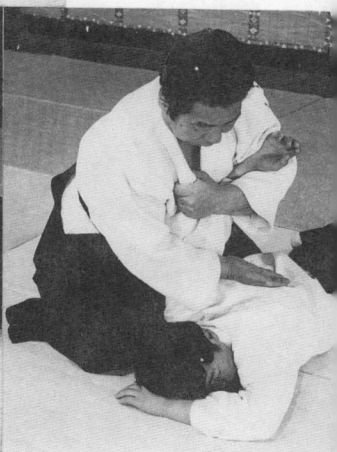

Shomen-uchi Dai-Nikyo Ura-waza

Hold your partner's wrist with your left hand, cut it downward with Tegatana as you turn your body obliquely to hold him captive and hold the back of his hand with your right hand. Then bend his arm in the shape of "<" as shown here, draw his elbow toward you causing his thumb to point at his nose and stimulate his wrist. This done, turn your body obliquely again, enmesh his elbow within your hold with Tegatana and finish off the exercise.

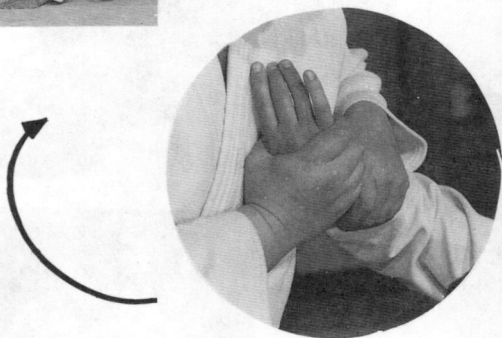

Mune-dori *(Lower lapel held)* Dai-Nikyo Ura-waza ⇨

This is one of a great many Ura-waza varieties. In this particular exercise, hold your collar with your left hand making a shift of hold to your right hand easier. Once the shift has been made, turn your body and stimulate your partner's wrist.

⇦ Mune-dori Dai-Nikyo Ura-waza

Unbalance your partner sideways by delivering Atemi, turn your hips in a Dai-Ikkyo manner and assume reverse oblique stance. In all modes of training, care must be taken to make your body movements immune from opposition attacks.

- **Dai-Sankyo** *(Arm twist)*

Shomen-uchi Dai-Sankyo Omote-waza

First, hold your partner down in the manner of Dai-Ikkyo Omote-waza. At this stage of the exercise, be careful about your right-hand hold. Following the "hold-down", advance your left foot to your partner's side, align yourself with him side by side and shift the hold to your left hand. Then take a forward step with your right foot while delivering Atemi to his face with your right hand, draw your left foot nearer and pin him down. In the process, your right hand slides down his elbow to wrist.

Shomen-uchi Dai-Sankyo Ura-waza

Ura-waza features aligning your toes and circularly pinning down your partner. As you bring yourself side by side with him, hold the back of his hand and circularly handle his momentum for a "hold-down".

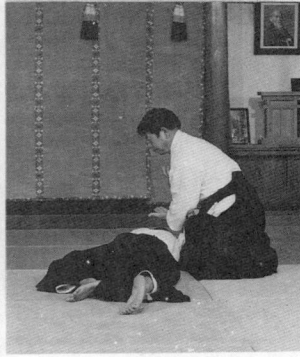

Dai-Sankyo Henka-waza *(Varied exercise)*

Slash your partner's face with Tegatana as you turn your body obliquely and land Atemi on his side chest with your left hand. Then knock down his parrying hand, switch the hold to your left hand and trigger Atemi to his face again with your right hand. His parrying momentum can be used to advantage as you slide past his side and launch a cutting motion. Orthodox Dai-Sankyo methods are applicable in holding your partner's hands and holding him down in this exercise.

Dai-Sankyo Henka-waza

The varied exercise introduced on the preceding page is concluded with a "hold-down". This varied exercise, however, features extension into a "throw". Dai-Sankyo variations are classified into two categories — 1) Gliding past your partner's side and 2) no such passage. The former may be called an inward rotary movement and the latter its outward version.

Tsuki *(Thrust)* Dai-Sankyo Henka-waza

If you were exposed to a frontal thrust attack, chop down the thrusting hand and follow up the action with basic Dai-Ikkyo or Dai-Sankyo techniques. This varied exercise is employed when the distance between you and your partner is close and you have to swing up his elbow while obliquely turning your body outside and resort to Dai-Sankyo techniques.

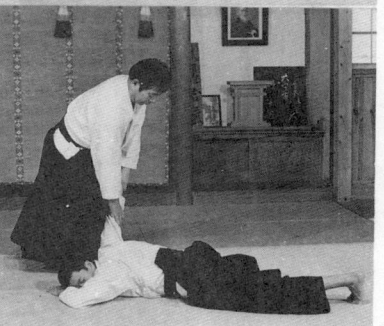

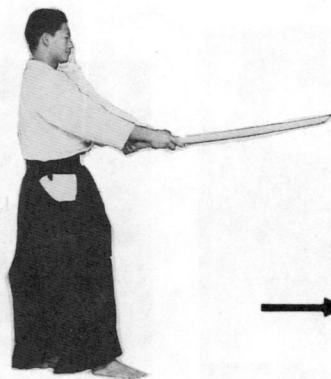

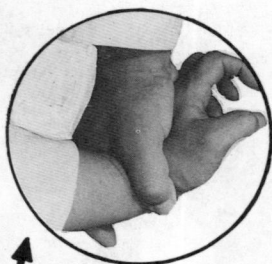

Tachi-dori *(Sword-taking)*

"Tachi-dori" is an exercise of taking a sword away from your partner and subduing him in a situation where he mounts an armed attack against you when you are empty-handed and thus defenseless. This Tachi-dori exercise is an applied form of Dai-Sankyo.

The beginner is far from qualified to take up Tachi-dori. This exercise could be extremely dangerous unless the trainee has had enough practice in Suburi and Awase (Matching of Ken) which make possible a good command of body movements. Even if you are capable of good body movements, there is a possibility of your being hit when you leave your hands and feet on the path of attack or wield the captured sword improperly.

"Even when you have Ken (Sword) with you, do not depend on it. Similarly, even when you have Jo (Stave) with you, do not consider it separate from your body".

This concept should be used to good advantage in Tachidori which is the stretched version of Awase and Kumi-tachi (Sword partnership).

→

- **Dai-Yonkyo** *(Forearm pin)*

Shomen-uchi Dai-Yonkyo Omote-waza

Dai-Yonkyo provides a good training method whereby the pulsating spot of the wrist is properly pressured. Such pressure is good for the health of the trainee who receives it. The pressure-giving trainee also benefits by learning a hold impregnated with hip power.

→

Shomen-uchi Dai-Yonkyo Ura-waza

This exercise features turning your body obliquely while pressuring your partner's wrist and circularly holding him down.

Tachi-dori

This is a Dai-Yonkyo version of Tachi-dori. As in the case of Dai-Sankyo Tachi-dori, place yourself alongside your partner and wrest the sword from his hand. While so doing, pressure his wrist on the pulse side.

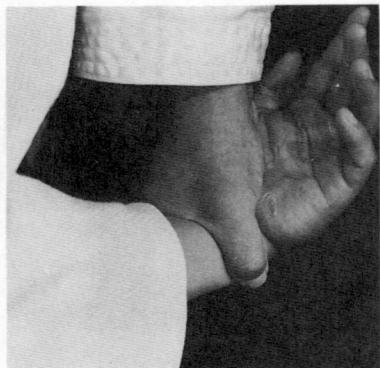

  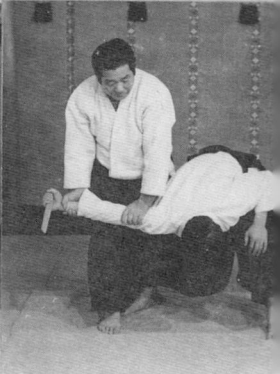

- Dai-Gokyo *(Defence against armed attacks)*

Yokomen-uchi *(Circular strike at the head)* Dai-Gokyo Omote-waza

Since this is a dagger-taking exercise, use of Dai-Ikkyo body movements is rather dangerous. In coping with the circular strike, it is necessary to step into the attacker's side, check his hand and hold him down by turning your hips fully "like the movement of the billows". The way his wrist is held is different from the Dai-Ikkyo version. In order to take the dagger which the attacker firmly holds, bend his arm as shown in the photo at left and bring pressure to bear on it from above, thus causing his fingertips to open automatically. Then kick the dagger away with your heel.

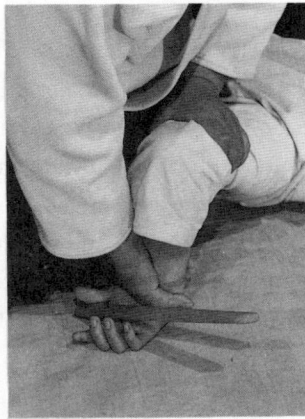

Yokomen-uchi Dai-Gokyo Ura-waza

This exercise calls for your striding to your partner's side to render the strike ineffectual, quickly aligning your toes and circularly holding him down as you turn your body obliquely. In countering the strike, you must knock it down really hard. Otherwise, you will be in danger. The photo at left illustrates this point.

Henka-waza *(Varied exercise)*

This exercise, although not considered part of the Go-Kyo category, is being introduced here because of its relevance to Yokomen-uchi on the preceding page. This is not Ura-waza as such since it involves both inward and outward body movements. In this exercise, it is important to secure a hold after knocking down the striking hand to the lowest possible level and immediately commence the "hold-down", blending harmoniously your body movements with your partner's.

4. Throwing exercise

Shiho-nage *(Four-corner throw)*

● Shiho-nage Omote-waza

Ken movements in Aikido really stand to reason. This particular Shiho-nage, with both hands held, is free from conflict with the opponent power and identical to Taijutsu. Hip turns and abdominal breath power are major elements common to Aikido Ken and Taijutsu. In this sense, both branches of the art are integrated.

(Principle of Ken)

Body movements in Aikido always presuppose multiple-attack. Photo shows a case of being attacked from the front and rear. First, cut down the front enemy and as you swing up the sword, make a clean sweep of his torso. Then, turn your body 270 degrees for a cutting counterattack on the rear attacker. This is the sequence of Shiho-nage Omote-waza explained in Japanese fencing terms.

Katate-dori *(One hand held)* Shiho-nage Ura-waza

Shiho-nage is so called because it is an exercise of throwing your partner in four directions. This is Ura-waza which features throwing your partner at your front.

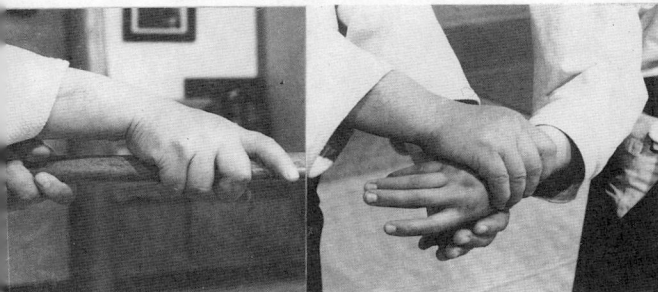

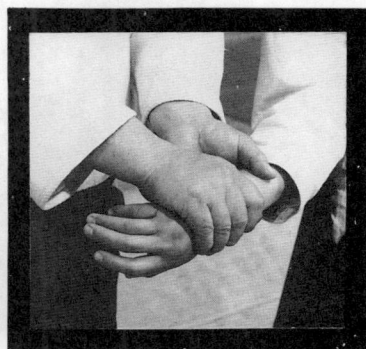

- **Irimi-nage** *(Entering throw)*

In Hanmi-Handachi (Sitting vs. Standing) Irimi-nage, "fold up" your partner for a throw. This training method can also be used in dealing with a taller opponent.

Shomen-uchi Irimi-nage

Irimi-nage is a combination of entry into the rear of your partner and a subsequent throw. Following the entry, pull him onto your chest, turn your hips in the manner of striking with Ken and throw him down. Irimi training methods are wide in variety and include the following:

1) Throwing with your left hand only; 2) Throwing with your right hand only; 3) Throwing combined with leading your partner's hand your way; 4) Throwing attempted when you are about to be hit; 5) Leading your partner's "Ki" and throwing him without using your hands.

These methods multiply as the exercises are carried out in a variety of standing, sitting and sitting vs. standing postures.

Tachi-dori

Irimi-nage is a secret means of successfully pulling out of a ring of many attackers. When the attacker is armed with a sword, it is necessary to throw him down and wrest the implement from him simultaneously. Otherwise, the situation is dangerous because there is no telling which way the sword may fly when you throw him. After seizing the sword, hold him in check at sword point.

Irimi-nage Henka-waza *(Varied exercise)*

This is an exercise of lifting your partner, his face looking upward, with your hands above your head. Perfect Irimi is required to make the exercise possible. Main emphasis should therefore be placed on Irimi in your training.

● Kotegaeshi *(Wrist turn-out)*

(Principle of Ken)

This exercise requires you to turn your partner's wrist out for a throw and hold him down. Let us suppose a situation in which you are flanked by front and rear enemies. How Kote-gaeshi fits into the picture may be explained in terms of Ken. First, turn your body obliquely for a sweeping cutting motion across the rear attacker's torso, following up the action with turning the front assailant's wrist out for a subsequent stroke.

Tachi-dori

If the little finger of your right hand is hooked onto the hilt of your partner's sword, you will find it easier to take the sword. Aikido exercises can be explained in terms both of the Japanese fencing art and Taijutsu. This may give the impression that the whole thing is rather complicated, but actually, understanding of it can be expedited as long as you have mastered such basic exercises as Suburi and Awase.

Tsuki *(Thrust)* Kotegaeshi

Kotegaeshi techniques are varied in number in Taijutsu applications. Such applications include cases of exposure to thrusting attacks or circular strikes at the head or dagger-taking. Kotegaeshi is based on how to hold the sword, the process of which begins with the small finger followed gradually by other fingers. In the case of Taijutsu, Atemi must be remembered as a matter of a preliminary must.

How to turn the wrist

Begin closing your grip with the little finger of each hand. Your right hand blends with the back of the opponent's.

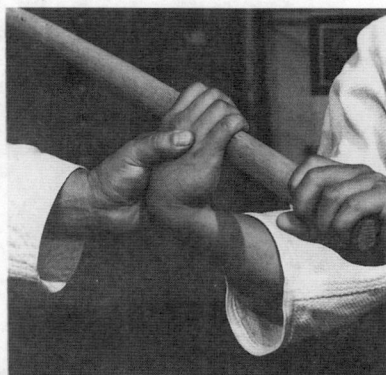

Kotegaeshi Varied Exercise No. 1

Katate-dori (One hand held) Kotegaeshi may be classified into two categories — 1) Disengaging your partner's hold in a fashion introduced on the preceding page and 2) the varied exercise introduced here. The latter features a method whereby you wrest your partner's thumb and hold him down for a throw.

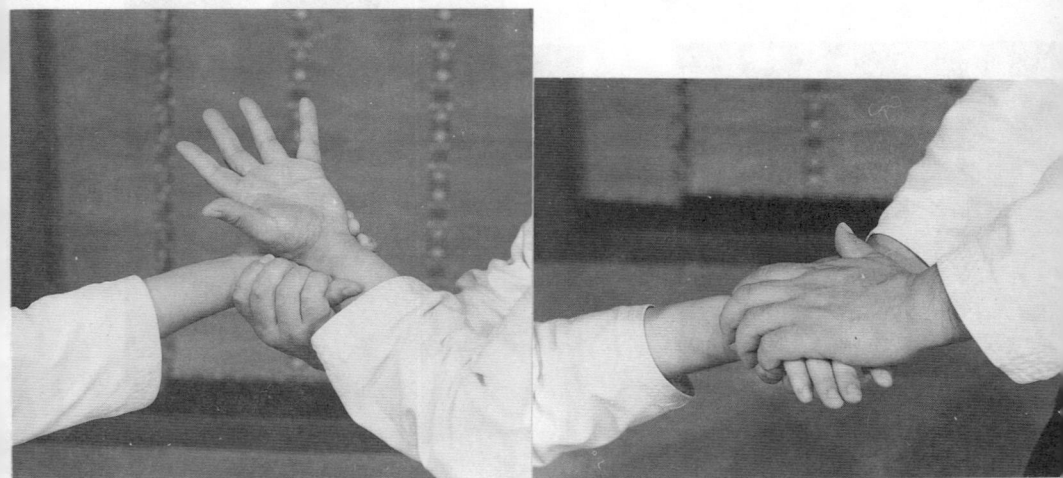

Kotegaeshi Varied Exercise No. 2

In case you are pulled toward your partner or he stays immobile at the time you try to turn his wrist out, take a step forward in keeping with the pulling momentum and initiate a throw. His arm and wrist are bent in the right direction but a spiral twist could, in its extreme form, cause a severe pain to him.

- **Koshi-nage** *(Hip throw)*

Mune-dori *(Lower lapel held)* Koshi-nage

Koshi-nage, which preconditions your hips combat- ready after deflecting your partner's striking attacks, has the following three rules that must be observed:

1) Lower your hips so that your arms may be fully stretched; 2) Look at your fingertips when you lower your hips for a stabilized posture; 3) Form a cross between you and your partner. When your fingertips are pointed vertically at the heaven, you are not in a position to form a cross pattern with your partner. The desired angle is about 45 degrees, which is attainable when your fingertips are directed at the top of a pillar or a wall. When throwing, it is a requisite to turn your hips to such a degree that you may see the fingertips of your opposite hand. The crossing point lies in your hips and your partner's navel, a spot where the load to be thrown is supposed to the lightest.

Ushiro Mune-dori *(Lower lapel held from behind)* Koshi-nage

This is basic Koshi-nage which is applied when you are held from behind. When your hands are held from behind, raise your hand in a Ken-swinging fashion and hug your partner's arm into your inner hold for a throw. As the next page shows, there is a way of throwing your partner away by getting hold of his wrist.

Varied exercise when pulled backward

When pulled backward, take a step back to realign your posture and cut him down for a throw.

In keeping with your partner's pulling momentum, bring yourself to his rear quickly as if causing your weight to descend on him and throw him down. Variations therefore are effected in harmony with his movements.

Ushiro Ryote-dori *(Both hands held from behind)* Nage-waza *(Throwing technique)*

It is recommended that Ushiro Ryote-dori be performed after the pattern of Ushiro Mune-dori (Lower lapel held from behind) Koshi-nage. Note that Koshi-nage can be transformed into a throwing exercise without any contact with your partner.

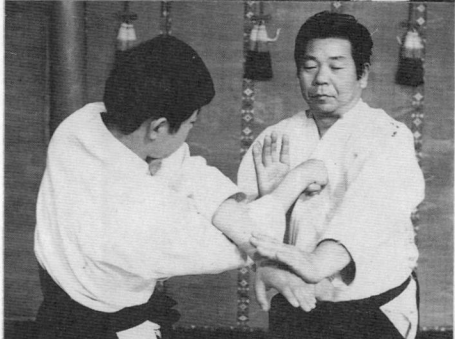

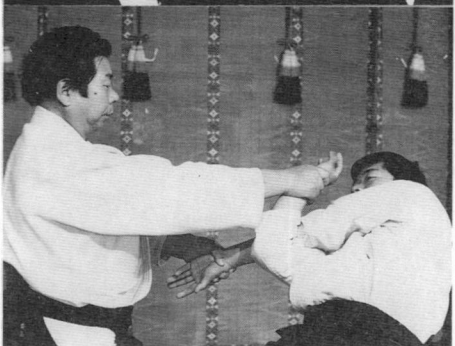

● Jyujigarami *(Cross-twine throw)*

Mune-dori *(Lower lapel held)* Jyuji-garami

The minute you have your lower lapel held, launch Atemi to your partner's face and lure his left hand out. Take that hand, entwine his elbows in the form of a cross and flip him away by extending your arms.

Ushiro Ryote-dori *(Both hands held from behind)* Jyujigarami

Swing up your left hand from in front of your navel as you move into your partner's side. When you are out of his hold, hold his both hands and entwine them in the shape of a cross for a throw.

● Kaiten-nage *(Rotary throw)*

(Inward Kaiten-nage)

As soon as your right hand is held, shoot Atemi at your partner's face. If the blow is parried outward, do not resist the counteraction but circularly step to his side. The circular pattern shown in this photo is called an inward rotary move. At the same time as you draw your right foot into place after entering your partner's side, initiate a cutting motion with your right Tegatana with your left hand bringing pressure to bear on his head to pull it toward you. Then stretch your right hand for a throw while firing Atemi at his face with your right knee.

Put your right foot forward to his side and then turn your body by advancing your left foot. As you draw your right foot in front of your left foot, it is desired that your foot posture form a triangular pattern.

121

● Tenchi-nage *(Heaven-earth throw)*

This exercise must assume the form of Irimi inasmuch as Irimi precludes your physically running into conflict with your partner. In practicing this exercise, your hands part their ways pointing at the heaven and earth, respectively. Hence the name "heaven-earth throw". The hands, however, do not remain separate forever. As this photo shows, it is significant to note that the hands are linked up again as a ring.

5. Flow of "Ki"

This exercise may best be practised in three different ways. The first method may be called rigid training (SOLID) in which you start functioning after having your hand or other parts of the body held by your partner. This is the so-called static-to-static exercise which is deliberately designed to encourage inflexible training.

The second method is flexible training (FLEXIBLE) which features both you and your partner being on the move. Flexible means, for instance, changing the angle of your hand held and thereby inducing a situation where a technique is easier to unleash. The third method is called "flow of Ki", a training formula which causes your partner's "Ki" to flow out (FLUID).

The Aikido Founder once described this as "training in the gravitation of the universe". An illustrious example of this is throwing your partner without coming into contact with him at all by calling out his "Ki" and linking it with yours. This is made possible by forming a curtain of "Ki" between his hands and yours. Photo below shows the type of Irimi-nage in which you turn your body obliquely for a throw in the face of an onrushing strike. Photo on the right page shows Irimi-nage featuring "flow of Ki" which calls out your partner's "Ki".

6. Happo-giri (eight-corner cutting)

Thi is an exercise of cutting in eight directions by hip and other body turns. The vital part of the exercise is the timing of turning your body 270 degrees in one quick sweep. (Photos 6, 7 and 8)